Choosing your
CLEMATIS

'Wada's Primrose' and 'Broughton Star' decorate a pergola.

Choosing *your*
CLEMATIS

John Howells

Photographs by the author
Consultant – Wim Snoeijer

GARDEN • ART • PRESS

ACKNOWLEDGEMENTS

As in previous books I have enjoyed enthusiastic support from my literary assistant, Mrs Janet Hodge, and the dedicated team at my publishers, the Antique Collectors' Club.

Authority has been given to the book by the availability of my consultant, Wim Snoeijer of the University of Leiden. Even with his help, errors may have crept into the book; for these the author is entirely responsible.

———————————

CONTENTS

Introduction

To be able to choose your clematis you need to know the choices available. But there are over 1,000 clematis on the market! So how can you know the features of 1,000? How can you tell one plant from the other?

I was bewildered too. But after study in 1992[1] it became apparent to me that all the clematis fell into a small number of groups, just twelve in all. Now I could easily know all the clematis. If I knew one clematis in a group then I could be sure that the others in that group were the same. So, if I knew one clematis from each of the twelve groups, twelve clematis in all, I could know the features of all clematis. All was now easy. This grouping caught on. Classifying in the twelve groups is now universally followed.

Another fact emerged, the twelve groups followed one another through the year – from winter, through spring, summer and autumn back to winter. I could now easily remember when each group, and its plants, flowered.

You need not be bewildered by 1,000 clematis on the market. Knowing just twelve clematis gives you the features of all twelve groups and thus all clematis. Knowing the twelve groups is the key to knowing clematis. Knowing the groups, you can easily tell what clematis to grow in your garden to give the effect that you want.

This book will show you each of the twelve groups. It will also describe three to six example plants in each group. Read about one group at a time, look at the examples, and you will quickly learn the features of that group. Soon you will know all twelve groups and so the whole of clematis.

The twelve groups, in approximate order of flowering, are:

I   The Evergreen Group – the tender group – Winter flowering
II   The Alpina Group – the group of single bells – Early Spring
        flowering
III   The Macropetala Group – the group of double bells –
        Early Spring flowering
IV   The Montana Group – the group of giant clematis –
        Spring flowering
V   The Rockery Group – the group of dwarf clematis –
        Spring flowering
VI   The Early Large Flowered Group – the 'dinner plate'
        group – Late Spring flowering
VII   The Late Large Flowered Group – the 'tea plate' group
         – Early Summer flowering
VIII   The Herbaceous Group – the border group – Early
        Summer flowering
IX   The Viticella Group – the easy group – Summer flowering
X   The Texensis Group – the group of climbing tulips –
        Late Summer flowering
XI   The Orientalis Group – the yellow group – Late
        Summer flowering
XII   The Late Group – the autumn group – Autumn flowering

The Key to Selecting a plant is to know the 12 Groups

The Book

Selecting your clematis will be discussed shortly. This will be helped by a
table of the seasons when the groups flower.

   The book will also tell you about the ways of buying clematis. It will also
tell you how to start a clematis collection. One, and only one, group is
effected by stem-rot (clematis wilt). This book will tell you about wilt and
knowing about it, you will see how you can easily manage it, should it occur.
Guides to pronouncing 'clematis' and to hardiness ratings follow while the
Appendix contains lists of clematis in colour choice and for special purposes.

REFERENCES
1. Howells, J. (1992) 'A Gardener's Classification of Clematis'. The Clematis, p.14.

'Fair Rosamond' climbs into a gazebo.

Selecting your Clematis

There are two useful rules:
I Select the GROUP of clematis first and then the plant.
II Select before you go to the nursery. (Failure to do this and you could be attracted to some beautiful clematis, fine in itself, but wrong for your purpose.)

Where in the garden do you propose to put your clematis?
The answer to this obvious question will help you answer the next questions.

When do you want it to flower?
Answers to this question will tell you the group that you need. (Check in the table SEASONS WHEN GROUPS FLOWER on page 11.) There may only be one group at that time of the year or there may be two or three in the months when there is rapid growth. Read up that group or groups in this book. Each time you do this you learn about what a particular group offers. After doing this a few times you will know the groups and not need to consult the descriptions.

Having decided the time of flowering, and thus the group or groups available at that time, you now need to ask some more questions of yourself:

How much space have I got?
You need to choose from the group the clematis of the right size for your space e.g. you have decided on Group XI, the orientalis group, for flowering in early autumn. You have space for the huge 'Bill Mackenzie'. Or you may only have space for 'Helios', a much smaller plant.

What colour do I want?
You may want a pink or a white to lighten a dark corner or a blue clematis to go with a yellow rose. Or you may just like a particular colour of clematis. Check under the group in the book to see if it has the colour of your choice, or for a larger choice, check in the table of that colour in the Appendix.

Do I have any special requirements?
You may want one from a group for a **north-facing wall**. Check the table of north-facing wall plants in the Appendix. Or you may want one for **semi-shade.** Those for the north-facing wall will suit semi-shade also. Or you may want a **scented** plant from that group. Check the table of scented flowers in the Appendix. Lastly you may find, regrettably, that you just do not have ground space and that the **container** is the best choice. So check the table of container plants in the Appendix for a plant in the group you want.

Examples.
1. Looking out of a window at a wall, you may wish that you had colour there in the winter. The possible answer lies with three groups: Group I – Evergreen, Group II – Alpina, Group III – Macropetala. If there is space *Clematis armandii* from Group I would be glorious – and give you wonderful scent. But if the space is smaller, the colour of your choice from the Alpina or Macropetala groups might be the answer. If you must have scent then you will settle for *C. alpina* 'Odorata'.

2. You want a clematis to match the flowering on a rose such as 'Compassion'. The rose flowers a long time – June to November. There are a number of groups available to you – Group VI – The Early Large Flowered, Group VII – The Late Large Flowered, Group IX – The Viticella Group and Group X – The Texensis Group. All will climb into your rose. After reading about the groups you may settle on one. Or as 'Compassion' is such a large rose, you may decide to grow three clematis into it – blue 'Lasurstern' from Group VI which flowers early, followed by pink 'Hagley Hybrid' from Group VII the Late Large Flowered[1] and followed by white 'Huldine' from the Viticellas, Group IX.[2]

3. Your garden is so dark in October, perhaps there is a clematis to light it up? You have two groups to choose from – Group XI the Orientalis, or Group XII the Late group. If you fancy a luminous yellow then 'Golden Tiara' from Group XI will see you through the month. But if scent is your need, then *Clematis terniflora* from Group XII would do a superb job as long as you have a sunny spot for it.

1. For early summer flowering.
2. For late summer flowering.

SEASONS WHEN GROUPS FLOWER

SEASON	N – Northern Hemisphere		S – Southern Hemisphere	
EARLY WINTER December N June S	Group I Evergreen			
MIDWINTER January N June S	Group I Evergreen			
LATE WINTER February N August S	Group I Evergreen			
EARLY SPRING March N September S	Group II Alpina	Group III Macropetala		
MID SPRING April N October S	Group II Alpina	Group III Macropetala	Group V Rockery	
LATE SPRING May N November S	Group IV Montana	Group V Rockery		
EARLY SUMMER June N December S	Group VI Early Large			
MIDSUMMER July N January S	Group VI Early Large	Group VII Late Large	Group VIII Herbaceous	Group IX Viticellas
LATE SUMMER August N February S	Group VII Late Large	Group VIII Herbaceous	Group IX Viticellas	Group X Texensis
EARLY AUTUMN September N March S	Group X Texensis	Group XI Orientalis		
MID AUTUMN October N April S	Group XI Orientalis	Group XII Late		
LATE AUTUMN November N May S	Group XII Late			

N.B.   1. Clematis in a group that are early or late flowering in that group will
                overlap with other groups
          2. The months with more light will have more choice of groups.

A REMINDER

In order to make the text useful in both hemispheres, plant flowering times, etc. are described in terms of seasons, not months. The following table translates seasons into months for the two hemispheres.

Northern Hemisphere		Southern Hemisphere
Midwinter	January	Midsummer
Late winter	February	Late summer
Early spring	March	Early autumn
Mid–spring	April	Mid–autumn
Late spring	May	Late autumn
Early summer	June	Early winter
Midsummer	July	Midwinter
Late summer	August	Late winter
Early autumn	September	Early spring
Mid–autumn	October	Mid–spring
Late autumn	November	Late spring
Early winter	December	Early summer

'Huvi' displays its structure of 3 circles: 1. The outer circle of six large purple tepals. 2. The middle tight circle of dark purple stamens. 3. The inner circle of prominent white carpels.

THE PARTS OF A CLEMATIS FLOWER

The make-up of anything depends on the use that is going to be made of it. In the case of a clematis flower its use is to make sure that there will be more clematis plants, otherwise clematis will disappear as a race.

To ensure the continuation of the human race, a male cell is required to come into contact with a female cell. This in turn forms a seed which, when planted into the womb of the female, will ultimately develop into another human being.

It is exactly the same in the clematis plant. We need a male cell, pollen grain (in the stamen) to meet a female cell (in the carpel). The two have to come together and make a seed that the wind will carry to plant in the ground and make a new clematis.

In clematis we also need something to carry the male cell (pollen grain) from the stamen to the female cell in the carpel. This is done by insects, attracted by colourful petals, who come to feed on the pollen. The pollen from that clematis, or another they have visited, clings to their bodies and these clinging cells may touch the sticky tip of the carpel when it is immediately pounced upon. It travels down the carpel and meets the female cell. The two cells come together in the carpel to make a seed.

So we need 1) petals to attract the insects; 2) stamens to supply male cells; 3) carpels to supply female cells. We can think of these three parts as circles.

A clematis flower may take many shapes but you will always have three circles – which we will now study.

CIRCLE 1 – Circle of tepals – the outside circle.

I have chosen, for study, the very attractive tulip-shaped flower of Clematis 'Duchess of Albany' from Group X, the Texensis Group – the group of climbing tulips. **Please take from your garden just one flower from a clematis plant and do what I do.**

Most flowers have a green sepal that protects the flower and a petal that attracts insects.

Clematis flowers are different in that the sepal does two jobs. It protects the flower like a sepal and attracts the insects with bright colours – like a petal. So it is given a special name – tepal. This is true of all clematis flowers.

In the outside circle as you can see are five brightly coloured tepals with the mouth opening to let the insects into the flower.

Your flower too will have a ring of colourful tepals.

CIRCLE 2 – Circle of Stamens – the middle circle.

I have taken away from the flower two tepals facing the camera. **If you like you can take off all the tepals from your flower.** We can now see inside the flower.

At the bottom end of the flower there is a circle of short thin stems – the stamens.

There are three parts to each stamen.
1. The long lower part is called the filament – yellowish-white here.
2. The anthers at the top – yellow here.
3. Between the anthers is the area called the connective – red here.

The important part is the anther for it produces many, many, male cells – the pollen grains.

If you look hard above the stamens you will see a white area. This is the circle of carpels we will study next.

Having taken the tepals away in your flower you will see the stamens. Pluck one stamen out, put it on white paper, and you will soon see its three parts.

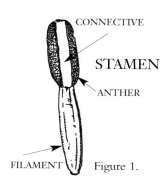

CONNECTIVE

STAMEN

ANTHER

FILAMENT

Figure 1.

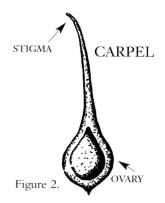

STIGMA

CARPEL

Figure 2.

OVARY

CIRCLE 3 – Circle of Carpels – the inside circle.

I have now taken away all of the stamens facing the camera. **You can take away some or all the stamens in your flower.** We can now see the tight circle of carpels at the very centre of the flower. There are a number of them, ten or more. Tightly packed together. Each is a silky white.

The tiny tip, the stigma, is sticky. A pollen grain sticks to this. Once one pollen grain is accepted, the door shuts and no more grains can enter.

The male cell slips down the stalk of the carpel, meets the female cell and in time forms a seed. Each flower can produce a number of seeds as there are a number of carpels. The seeds will float away on the wind, find soil, and so more clematis flowers are made.

You can take one carpel out of the bunch and you will see the tiny, sticky stigma at the very top.

For us, clematis are grown for their attractive shape, colour and scent. For the flowers, the serious business of making seeds is now over – and so they die. We humans likewise, though we do try to achieve rather more than merely making seeds!

GROUP I
THE EVERGREEN GROUP
The Tender Group

The first group to flower. Though tender, these large, sometimes scented, clematis are a miracle of winter flowering. They flourish on outside sheltered walls. But they are dramatic given plenty of room in a conservatory. They dislike a cold wind even more than a low temperature. They are evergreen in winter – winter green.

Flowering time:	Late autumn and winter indoors; late winter out of doors.
Size:	Can make very large plants covering an area up to 20 sq.m.
Strength:	Once established they make rapid growth.
Flowers:	Open bells of intensely scented blooms of *C. armandii* and *C. paniculata* and hanging bells of *C. cirrhosa* and *C. napaulensis*. Predominant colour is white.
Leaves:	Much variation here from parsley-like fine foliage of *C. cirrhosa* and *C. napaulensis* to the large thick leaves of *C. armandii*.
Care:	These plants have a dormant period in the summer; will lose some or all their foliage, particularly *C. napaulensis*. No pruning.
Uses:	On walls in sheltered positions; climbing into large trees; conservatories.
Points for:	Winter flowering. Plenty of flowers, some scented. Large plant. No particular pest or disease. Free of stem rot (clematis wilt).
Points against:	Tender. Too large for small gardens.
Hardiness ratings:	USA – Zones 6-9. Worldwide – average annual minimum temperature – above -23°C (-10°F)

C. armandii 'Apple Blossom' at Killerton, Devon, UK.

C. armandii 'Apple Blosssom' with red *Cydonia japonica*.

C. armandii
'Apple Blossom'

Hardiest Evergreen. First choice. Open flower in clusters. Pinky-white with mauve-pink at back of tepal. Strong vanilla or haw-thorn scent. Thick dark green glossy leaves, bronze when young.

Buds.

C. cirrhosa 'Freckles'

C. cirrhosa **'Freckles'**

This plant comes from the Mediterranean. In the wild its leaves and the colouring of its flowers can vary greatly from plant to plant, within yards of one another. Each form gets a name according to its attributes. For example, amount of freckles gives the name 'Freckles'; colour as in 'Wisley Cream'; shape of leaves in var. *tribola*, etc. Hanging bells. Greeny-white tepals with red-maroon blotches. Green stamens. Finely cut leaves, parsley-like. Fluffy seed heads.

Seed heads.

Clematis napaulensis flower.

Clematis napaulensis

Has similarities to *C. cirrhosa* but is more tender. Flowers early winter. Long hanging greenish-white bells. Attractive long purple stamens peeping below bell.

Bright green finely cut leaves.

Clematis paniculata (female flower).

Clematis paniculata

Needs a conservatory in cold areas. Scented flowers in spring. Gives a spectacular display once established on a plant up to 15ft. (4.5m.). Male plant has orange pink anthers, female has a boss of green carpels. Thick glossy small leaves.

Clematis paniculata leaf.

GROUP II
THE ALPINAS

The Group of Single Bells

These clematis of single nodding bells, from the mountains, are the Heralds of Spring. They are very hardy, even to growing on a north-facing wall. Of manageable size, they look gorgeous hanging down a low wall. If it is still cold out there, position them where you can see them from your windows. (Alpina – from the alpine zone.)

Flowering time:	The early spring onwards.
Size:	Area of up to 10 sq. ft. (3 sq. m.). Height up to 8 ft. (2.4 m.).
Strength:	Very hardy. Make growth with ease.
Flowers:	Single bells of about 2 in. (5 cm.) length, in a big range of colours. Fine seed heads until the winter. (See 'Constance'.) No scent.
Leaves:	Attractive small soft green leaves with three lobes. (See 'Blue Dancer'.)
Care:	Plant like any shrub. No special pests or diseases. No pruning.
Uses:	Growing down a small wall. Climbing into low shrubs and small trees. In containers. Over rockeries.
Points for:	Easy to grow. Very hardy. Flower when little else gives colour. Fine range of colours. Good seed heads. Free of stem rot (clematis wilt).
Points against:	No yellows. No scent. ('Odorata' an exception)
Hardiness ratings:	USA – Zones 3-9. Worldwide – average annual minimum temp. above -40°C (-40°F)

C. alpina 'Ruby' climbs into a rose bush.

Alpina 'Blue Dancer'.

'Blue Dancer' (syn. Francis Rivis)

The first choice in this group for its elegance, size of bloom, and its clear light blue-mauve tepals with contrasting white stamens. Makes a nodding bell with slightly twisted tepals each about 2-2½in. (5-6cm.) long.

Alpina 'Blue Dancer' single.

Alpina 'Blue Dancer' leaf.

Clematis 'Jacqueline du Pré' with Saxifraga.

'Jacqueline du Pré'

Appeals for its large size of bloom. Attractive contrasting colours of tepals with exterior of rosy-mauve and interior of pale pink. Silver-pink margin to tepals. White stamens flecked with pink.

'Rosy Pagoda'

A free flowing alpina with attractive rosy-pink tepals. Stamens flecked with pink.

'Constance'

Appeals for its bright pinky-red tepals with ruffled surface. Semi-double flower. Very free with its flowering.

'Pink Flamingo'

The large flower of this alpina has pink tepals with red veins. Flower is semi-double. Appeals for its long flowering period.

'Columbine'

This elegant alpina has pale blue tepals with white stamens.

GROUP III
THE MACROPETALAS
The Group of Double Bells

These clematis of double nodding bells are only slightly later into bloom than the alpinas. Double bells allow a contrast in colour between the inner and outer bell and so give more interest than the alpinas. But some prefer the elegance of the single bell of the alpinas. A somewhat larger plant than the alpinas, very hardy and suitable for a north-facing wall and semi-shade. Very lovely hanging down on a low wall. They give colour when there is little else in the garden. (Macropetala = large petals.)

Flowering time:	Mid spring onwards
Size:	Up to 10ft. (3m.) in height.
Strength:	Very hardy. Will grow in poor soil, even in semi-shade and on north-facing walls.
Flowers:	Double bells up to 2⅜in. (6cm.) across. In a range of colours — purple, mauve, blue, pink, white. Fine seed heads into winter. (See *Clematis macropetala*.)
Leaves:	Attractive small green leaves. See 'Markham's Pink'.
Care:	Easy. Plant as any shrub. No particular disease or pest. No pruning.
Uses:	Down low walls. Up walls and pillars. Into shrubs and small trees. In containers. Over rockeries. In north-facing aspects and semi-shade.
Points for:	Easy to grow. Very colourful. Very hardy. Flowers when little colour elsewhere in the garden. Fine range of colours. Good seed heads.
Points against:	No yellows. No scent.
Hardiness ratings:	USA – Zones 3-9. Worldwide – average annual minimum temp. above -40°C (-40°F)

Clematis macropetala climbs up a pillar in the renowned rose garden of Mottisfont Abbey, Hampshire, UK.

'Markham's Pink'

This has a most attractive double pink flower. The outer bell of four tepals is dark pink. The inner bell of thinner tepals has the same colouring as the pale underside of the outer bell. Named after a famous clematarian, Ernest Markham. The stamens are creamy-white. The plant is covered in bloom which is followed by fluffy seed heads.

Clematis macropetala

This is the type plant (original from the wild) of the group and is most desirable. The outer bell of four tepals is a deep blue. The inner thin tepals making the inner bell are of a similar colour with flecks of white. The white stamens contrast beautifully with the blue tepals making an eye-catching flower. Very floriferous. Very reliable.

'Jan Lindmark'

This striking dark purple flower is from Sweden, striking not only for its colour but for the inner bell of tepals which are numerous, thin, are laced with white and project at all angles. The stamens are creamy-green. It flowers early.

'Rosy O'Grady'

A macropetala from Canada, which guarantees its hardiness. Being pink it has a likeness to 'Markham's Pink'. Here however the inner and outer bells are a different pink – the inner being lighter.

'Purple Spider'

This is well named. Not only are both bells of a deep purple but the flower holds itself in such a way as to give the impression of motion. The stamens are white flecked with purple.

'White Swan'

The cream bud opens to make a white double flower. The inner bell of tepals are irregular. The yellow anthers harmonise with the white tepals. A strong grower with light green foliage.

GROUP IV
THE MONTANAS
The Group of Giant Clematis

When these giant clematis spring into colour in late spring, the garden is set alight. They are probably the best-known clematis of all for their massive impact. They make such a colourful show that it is possible to forget the three groups that appeared earlier in the year. Each, singly, has a short period of flowering but by growing a few in succession (see below) they can give flower for a long time. (Montana = of the mountains.)

Flowering time:	Late spring and early summer.
Size:	Can grow up to 40ft. (12m.) and above, even up to the top branches of massive trees. However, some are small enough for small gardens.
Strength:	Very vigorous. Hardy except for frost damage.
Flowers:	Covered with a profusion of small open flowers about 2-2⅖in. (5-6cm.). Some are scented. Usually single flowers but there are a few with double flowers. Pink and white predominate as colours.
Leaves:	See 'Broughton Star'.
Care:	Plant as any other shrub. Make sure you have enough room for it. Flowers and sometimes leaves can be damaged by late frosts. No disorders or pests particular to it. No pruning.
Uses:	To cover walls, pillars, fences, roof of shed, into large trees (even evergreens).
Points for:	Wonderful mass of colour. Easy to grow. Some scented. Free of stem rot (clematis wilt).
Points against:	Short period of flowering, therefore grow a number with successive periods of flowering, e.g. 'Mayleen' 'Grandiflora' – *C. chrysocoma* – *C. chrysocoma* 'Continuity' – 'Peveril'. Frost damage: over small montanas and lower parts of large montanas hang garden fleece when frost threatens. No leaves in winter; therefore plant in places not visible from your windows.
Hardiness Zones:	USA – Zone 7-9. Worldwide – average annual minimum temp. above -18°C (0°F)

A *clematis montana* climbs high into a tall holly tree.

'Mayleen'

A giant amongst giants. I give pride of place to this montana for its size, vigour, ease of growth and large open pink flowers with gorgeous vanilla scent.

'Freda'

Ideal for a small garden. It has a deep pink flower. At first the flower is deep pink throughout but later the centre part becomes lighter. Dark bronze leaves. A striking plant.

'Grandiflora'

Another giant. Can cover a large area. Clear white flowers, freely produced. Easy to grow. A wonderful plant.

Clematis chrysocoma

Related to *C. montana* but flowers later. Downy hairs on leaves and stems. White flowers flecked with pink. Climbs up to 10ft. (3m.) and suitable for small garden. Long flowering. A fine plant.

'Broughton Star'

Best double montana. Four outside tepals
are unusual shade of reddy-orange. Inner
circle of many tepals of a deeper colour. A
profusion of flowers. Can make a plant up
to 14ft. (4.5m).

Clematis chrysocoma '**Continuity**'

A neglected treasure. A plant for every garden. Flowers even later than *C. chrysocoma* and thus extends even more the length of flowering in this group. Pink blooms on long stems with attractive eye-catching yellow stamens. Grows up to about 10ft. (3m.). Suitable for a small garden. You must have this one!

GROUP V
THE ROCKERY GROUP
The Group of Dwarf Clematis

In late spring at the feet of the giant clematis, believe it or not, are some of the most beautiful clematis you will ever see. They are a fascinating new interest in the world of clematis which up to now has been confined to alpine gardeners. These gems are of great loveliness and interest. A special interest perhaps but likely to appeal to many. A serious gardener may grow them in an alpine greenhouse. As an introduction to this dwarf world I suggest you start with the dwarf New Zealand clematis. These are unusual in having male and female plants. The alpinas and macropetalas, additional New Zealand plants, and a few small clematis can also be used on rockeries.

Flowering time:	Mid and late spring.
Size:	Plants as small as 1sq. ft. (30sq. cm.) or up to 2sq. ft. (60sq.cm.).
Strength:	Not hardy in cold climates.
Flowers:	Small open flowers up to 1in. (2.5cm.) wide. Many blooms. White and cream colours predominate. Followed by unusually fine seed heads. No scent.
Leaves:	Evergreen. (See *clematis marmoraria*)
Care:	Do best in acid, well-drained compost.
Uses:	Can be grown in the greenhouse and brought out when they flower to adorn beds, patios, flower boxes and hanging baskets.
Points for:	Unusual, attractive, flowers. Fine seed heads. Free of stem rot (clematis wilt).
Points against:	Not completely hardy. No scent. Do not grow as a climber.
Hardiness ratings:	USA – Zone 7-9. Worldwide – average annual minimum temp. above -18°C (0°F)

A gorgeous example of a New Zealand hybrid in a pot.

'Joe'

This is a wonderful New Zealand plant that was introduced in Scotland and named after the New Zealand hybridist, Joe Cartmann. Hardy only in a warm climate or very sheltered areas in a cold climate. Does best in a greenhouse or conservatory. Does not climb. Can hang down from a low wall, window boxes, hanging baskets or allowed to make a mound of bloom in a bed. There is a related female form, 'Early Sensation'. Keep in place to enjoy the gorgeous seed heads. Flowers can make up to 1½in. (4cm.) in width. The seed heads of the female form is shown.

Clematis marmoraria

This is the smallest clematis of all — the gem of gems. It comes from the Marble Mountains of New Zealand. Leaves are like parsley leaves and only rise 4–5in. (10-5cm.) from the ground. Most attractive buttercup like flowers about ¾ in. (2cm.) wide and coloured cream. It may take three to four years before it flowers. But worth waiting for and the spectacular seed heads are things of delicate beauty.

'Fairy'

The New Zealand clematis have been crossed with one another and crossed again producing a number of lovely hybrids. This is one. Lovely creamy-yellow flowers and gorgeous seed heads to follow in this female plant. As this is a female plant a tuft of carpels can be seen.

'Pixie'

'Pixie' also results from the crossing of New Zealand clematis. This male plant has an attractive greeny-cream colouring. Being a male plant the stamens are prominent.

GROUP VI
THE EARLY LARGE FLOWERED GROUP
The 'Dinner Plate' Group

This is the most striking group for size of flowers. The plants have large, shapely, colourful blooms. This is the group you will see most often at nurseries. Well over 500 different clematis of this group are available. Unhappily the flowers have a flaw. They are all susceptible to stem rot (clematis wilt). However, that should not prevent you from buying and growing them. At the end of the book there is a section telling you how to prevent and manage the wilt. These clematis are so beautiful, they are well worth the small amount of additional effort. The flowers appear on stem growth made the previous year. Here recommended for your trial are a few beauties that are said to be less susceptible to wilt than most. However, no guarantee can be given that they will not wilt. No two gardeners would pick the same list.

Flowering time:	Early to midsummer with often an extra flush in early autumn.
Size:	This is variable. Some to 6ft. (1.8m.), some to 8ft. (2.4m.) and some to 10ft. (3m.).
Strength:	Hardy. Will lose leaves in winter.
Flowers:	They can be single, semi-double and double. Some are stripped. Flower size is variable up to 10in. (25cm.). Very few have scent. Some have attractive seed heads.
Leaves:	Usually three leaflets (ternate).
Care:	Plant as any shrub. Most like plenty of sun and good watering into the ground (not on the leaves). Some will grow in semi-shade and on a north-facing wall. Prune out dead stems before flowering and burn. After flowering remove two thirds of each stem.
Uses:	On walls, fences, arches, pergolas, arbours; into shrubs, trees and roses; in containers.
Points for:	Their beauty. Their size. The large choice.
Points against:	Stem rot (clematis wilt). No scent. No true yellows (a few creamy-yellow).
Hardiness ratings:	USA – Zone 4-9. Worldwide – Average annual minimum temp. above -34°C (-30°F)

'Guernsey Cream', flowers early, and is climbing into a gazebo.

'Lasurstern'

This German flower displays the wonderful contrast of creamy-yellow stamens against the deep clear blue of the tepals. A crinkly edge adds to its attraction. One of the first to flower. A truly handsome flower.

Young bloom.

'Nelly Moser'

This French beauty is a survivor from the last century and still greatly admired. As the bud opens the incomparable delicate beauty of the flower unfolds. As it matures the flower fades in the sun. Thus it can be grown in semi–shade with profit. Tepals are pale mauve with reddy–lilac central bar. The anthers are dark red.

Mature flower.

'Elsa Späth'

A German clematis that is a good representative of the deep mauve-coloured clematis. Once established it is covered in bloom and repeats the display in the autumn. Reddish-purple anthers.

'Niobe'

Red clematis are popular and this Polish clematis could be the best. The red of the tepals is so deep as to be almost black at first opening. Velvety sheen to the flower. Greenish–yellow stamens. If hard pruned can be treated as Late Large Flower group.

'Miss Bateman'

This lovely British example from the last century is one of the most striking of all clematis. The white tepals contrast wonderfully with a large central eye of reddish–purple stamens. One of the first to flower and, for this reason, has an attractive tinge of green.

'Dr Ruppel'

Argentina has produced this hugely popular clematis. Some striped clematis can be garish but not this one. Gorgeous colouring of rosy-pink tepals with a deeper rosy-pink stripe. Light brown anthers.

GROUP VII
THE LATE LARGE FLOWERED GROUP
The 'Tea Plate Group'

Though the flowers here are not as big as the 'Early' group they are still of a medium size. However, they provide more colour than the 'Early' group because of the quantity of flowers. Some of the plants produce a volume of flowers almost matching those of a montana. Clematis wilt (stem rot) can make an occasional appearance but so seldom as not to merit special measures. Powdery mildew can appear in a bad year but is easily and speedily cured. Flowers appear on growth made the year of flowering.

Flowering time:	From midsummer onwards.
Size:	Can make plants up to 16ft. (5m.).
Strength:	Hardy. Reliable.
Flowers:	Very floriferous. Long flowering. Usually single open flowers. No scent. A range of colours except yellow.
Leaves:	Usually simple and pinnate.
Care:	Plant as any shrub. At first sign of powdery mildew spray with systemic fungicide of which there are many on the market. Pruning – I advocate to ground level in late winter.
Uses:	Up walls, pillars, arches, pergolas; on shrubs, small trees and climbing roses; some fit for containers.
Points for:	Vigour. Amount of bloom. Range of colours. Ease of growing.
Points against:	No scent. No yellows. Occasional powdery mildew.
Hardiness ratings:	USA – Zone 3-9. Worldwide – average annual minimum temp. above -40°C (-40°F)

'Perle d'Azur', like most clematis in this group, can make a large plant.

'Victoria'

One of the best clematis of all. Deep mauve tepals with rosy central bar. Makes a lot of flower. Very reliable. Highly recommended.

'Perle d'Azur'

The world's most popular clematis. Makes a very large plant. A lighter blue than most clematis though the colour proves to be a violet. Can be slow to start but do not let that deter you. Buy a strong plant.

'Hagley Hybrid'

One of the easiest clematis to grow. A bloom of delicate beauty when it opens. Shell pink tepals. Keeps to about 6ft. (1.8m.). Profusion of flowers. May fade in full sun. Good container plant.

'Gipsy Queen'

Classic deep mauve colour with a dark centre. Many flowers and climbs up to 10ft. (3m.). A showy plant.

'Comtesse de Bouchaud'

This clematis has been a favourite for over a hundred years. A lovely pink that fades a little as the flower matures.

'Madame Edouard André'

One of the best of the reds. Very reliable. Flowers over a long period.

GROUP VIII
THE HERBACEOUS GROUP
The Border Group

As the climbing clematis look for support to reach for the sun, there is activity at their feet in your border. Here you have your perennial plants and your shrubs. With them you can have no fewer than three sub-groups of border clematis. The first creep and clamber. The second are short upright plants. The third are tall upright plants. Each group is different, each is easy to grow, and each gives splendid colour.

Sub-group 1 – The Creepers – (The Heracleifolias)

These crawl, creep and clamber amongst your border plants. Most of them are very strong growing. They make a lot of leaf — large and coarse. A few have too much leaf and too little flower. The flower looks a bit like a hyacinth and can be scented. (Heracleifolia = having leaves like cow parsley.)

Heracleifolias

Flowering time:	Midsummer onwards
Size:	Not tall, some will cover an area of 10sq. ft. (3sq. m.)
Strength:	Hardy.
Flowers:	Usually a shade of blue but can be pink or white. At close inspection can remind you of a hyacinth. Some are deeply scented. Some have good seed heads (e.g. 'Côte d'Azur').
Leaves:	Large and coarse.
Care:	Plant as any shrub. Rich feeding. Will usually prune itself. Remove growth up to base in late winter.
Uses:	To add colour to your border. As ground cover. Will climb up walls and trees if required.
Points for:	Strong grower. Colour in borders. No stem rot (clematis wilt). Good seed heads.
Points against:	Sometimes too much leaf. Too vigorous for small areas. Small colour range.
Hardiness ratings:	USA Zone 3-9. Worldwide – average annual minimum temp. above -40°C (-40°F)

68

'Mrs Robert Brydon' displays the typical clambering habit of this sub-group. Here it almost engulfs border roses.

'Mrs. Robert Brydon'

A very vigorous, trouble-free plant. It is so vigorous and easy to grow that it can find its way into other named plants of this group. A white tubular bloom with violet patches.

Clematis x *jouiniana* 'Praecox'

The best ground cover clematis. Makes a very large plant. Will grow in any soil. The flowers are white tinged with violet. Has more flower than leaves and thus gives an excellent showy display. Flowers a long time. A very fine plant.

Sub-group 2 – Upright and Short – (The Integrifolias)

This is a splendid sub-group for the border. Makes clumps with upright flowers – of a great variety of colours. The bloom makes an attractive bell. They flower over a long period. (Integrifolia = having entire leaves.)

Flowering time:	Early summer onwards.
Size:	Up to 3ft. (1m.) in height.
Strength:	Hardy. Reliable.
Flowers:	Bells that are blue, red, pink, white. Makes very attractive seed heads. (See 'Rosea').
Leaves:	Characteristic simple leaves opposite one another on the stem without leaf having a stalk.
Care:	Plant as any shrub. Likes rich feeding. Prunes itself to the ground in the winter. Looks best with support from the many border supports available.
Uses:	For borders.
Points for:	Intrinsic beauty of flowers. Hardy. Long flowering. Immune from stem rot (clematis wilt).
Points against:	No yellows.
Hardiness ratings:	USA – Zone 3-9. Worldwide – average annual minimum temp. above -40°C (-40°F)

Clematis integrifolia 'Rosea' demonstrates the short upright growth of this sub-group.

'Rosea'

Possibly the Queen of the integrifolias. Gorgeous rosy-pink blooms sitting proudly on the stems. Scented.

PETIT FAUCON

Another very handsome plant. Nodding bells of deep blue. Excellent contrast of yellow stamens. As the tepals twist and curve a most attractive effect is produced.

Sub-group 3 – Tall and Upright – (The Diversifolias)

This group can add striking colour to a border — and for a long period. They are tall and commanding. (Diversifolia = having forms of different leaves.)

Flowering time:	Early summer onwards. Some flower for very long periods.
Size:	Up to 8ft. (2.4m.).
Strengths:	Very hardy.
Flowers:	Usually a profusion of flowers. Bloom often a bell or tubular shape. Mostly a shade of blue. No scent.
Leaves:	Variable.
Care:	Plant as any shrub. Support gives a tall column effect. Die to the ground each winter. Tidy in late winter.
Uses:	With support in borders. Can clamber through shrubs and trees.
Points for:	Beauty and amount of bloom. Vigour. Long flowering period. Trouble free. Immune to stem rot (clematis wilt).
Points against:	No scent. No yellows.
Hardiness ratings:	USA – Zone 3-9. Worldwide – average annual minimum temp. above -40°C (40°F)

'Blue Boy', the hardy clematis from Canada portrays the tall erect habit of this group.

'Durandii'

Could be regarded as the most beautiful bloom in the clematis world! The shape
is intriguing — large, bell-like but changing from flower to flower. Striking
yellow stamens, contrasting indigo-blue tepals and long firm stems produce a
stunning effect. Does not cling. Long flowering. A plant for every garden. Very
lovely as a cut flower.

'Hendersonii'

Full name is *clematis* x *eriostemon* 'Hendersonii'. The flowers are bell-like, of a deep purple, and cover the plant. Can flower for three months. Can be given support for erect display or allowed to clamber into shrubs. An easy, rewarding plant. Good for a container.

GROUP IX
THE VITICELLAS
The Easy Group

These clematis are so easy to grow that it is the obvious group for the gardener to try first. The flowers tend to appear as nodding bells that open out. Some blooms are of medium size but most are smaller. The flowers come in their hundreds and make sheets of colour. If you come across the wild viticella do grow it. It is lovely. (Viticella = small vine).

Flowering time:	Midsummer onwards. Some flower into the autumn.
Size:	Up to 15ft. (4.5m.).
Strength:	Very hardy.
Flowers:	Tend to be nodding bells that open flat. All colours except yellow. No scent — except the wild viticella and one other. Seed heads are not exciting.
Leaves:	Smaller and more divided than the Large Flowered.
Care:	Plant as any shrub. Will grow in semi-shade and north-facing walls. Fertilise well as it makes a lot of flower every year. Can have powdery mildew in a bad year and spray at once if seen. Prune to 3ft. (1m.) in the autumn, bring stems together with a tie; prune to the ground in late winter.
Uses:	Everywhere. On walls, fences, poles, pillars, pergolas; through shrubs, trees and climbing roses, over ground cover.
Points for:	Vigour. Reliability. Sweeps of colour. Ease of growth. No stem rot (clematis wilt).
Points against:	No yellows. Few scented. Poor seed heads.
Hardiness ratings:	USA – Zone 4–9. Worldwide – average annual minimum temp. above -40°C (-40°F).

'Margot Koster' climbs strongly over a holly hedge.

'Etoile Violette'

Same colouring as the old *jackmanii* but preferred by many to it. Showy flower of deep purple with contrasting creamy stamens. Flowers early. A fine plant.

'Madame Julia Correvon'

Another early bloomer. Flowers of rich red tepals have a contrasting light centre of creamy stamens. After the first flowering cut to half its height and it will flower again.

'Abundance'

So well named and lives up to it. Attractive red tepals with a violet tinge. Ruffled surface. Light centre of yellow stamens.

'Blue Belle'

It is purple rather than blue. Stamens are a contrasting yellow. Makes a pleasing flower. Large flower. Flowers late — into autumn and useful for this asset. Very vigorous.

'Minuet'

Flower is white with pink edge. In the breeze it dances (in this group there is also 'Tango' and 'Foxtrot'). A delightful clematis.

'Huldine'

Very well-regarded, well-shaped, elegant flower. White tepals tinged with violet. Broad violet central strip on back that makes it attractive viewed from behind. Long firm stalk that makes it good for cutting. Flowers late and into autumn.

There are many more viticellas, all excellent.

Try:
'Alba Luxurians' – green and white
'Betty Corning' – scented bell
'Kermesina' – red
'Little Nell' – white and violet
'Margot Koster' – deep pink
'Polish Spirit' – purple
'Purpurea Plena Elegans' – double
'Royal Velours' – deep red
'Venosa Violacea' – unusual colouring

GROUP X
THE TEXENSIS GROUP
The group of Climbing Tulips

This is probably the most beautiful single group in clematis. It is a small group – but each flower is a beauty. Upright tulips dancing in the breeze. This group can climb anywhere if you wish but it enjoys scrambling over shrubs, roses and small trees. Each has its supporters; all are attractive. (Texensis = from Texas, USA).

Flowering time:	Late summer onwards. 'Etoile Rose' flowers a month earlier.
Size:	Up to 8ft. (2.4m.). 'Etoile Rose' and 'Duchess of Albany' can make 12ft. (3.5m.).
Strength:	Hardy. Die to the ground in winter.
Flowers:	The plant can be covered with bloom. Most look upwards. 'Etoile Rose' hangs down. 4-6 tepals. No scent. All have glowing shades of pink or red. Good seed heads.
Leaves:	Glossy. Smooth. Often heart-shaped.
Care:	Plant as any other shrub. Likes a sunny place and rich feeding. Liable to powdery mildew; as soon as buds appear give a fortnightly spray of fungicide. Can tidy in the autumn by cutting off all but 3ft. (1m.) of stems and bringing these together with a tie. Complete pruning to the ground in late winter.
Uses:	Up poles, arches, pergolas, clambering over shrubs and small trees, as cut flowers on patios, for cutting.
Points for:	Intrinsic beauty. Colour in late summer.
Points against:	No scent. Powdery mildew (easily cured).
Hardiness ratings:	USA – Zone 4-9. Worldwide – average annual minimum temp. above -34°C (-30°F).

'Etoile Rose' hangs down from a 6ft. (1.8m.) support in a border, making a waterfall effect.

'Etoile Rose'

The outside of the tepal is pinky-red with a broad silvery-white margin. The inside is pink with a silvery-pink edge and ruffled surface. Yellow stamens. Earliest to flower, it is long-flowering and has nodding trumpets. Can climb to 12ft. (3.5m.).

'Duchess of Albany'

The outside of the tepal has a central white area suffused with pink and pink edge. The inside is pinky-violet, lighter at the edge. Anthers are yellow with deep mauve connective. Flower has a fine thick stalk and does not nod.

91

'Ladybird Johnson'

Outside of tepal is a dark red with broad silver strip to edge. The inside is deep red with crimson central stripe and ruffled surface. Yellow stamens.

'Princess Diana'

Outside of tepal is vivid pinky-red with silvery-white edge. Inside of tepal is again a vivid pinky-red which is lighter at edge. Yellow stamens. Look upwards.

'Sir Trevor Lawrence'

Outside of tepal is a silvery and red satiny mixture. The inside is crimson. Yellow stamens.

'Gravetye Beauty'

Latest to flower. Outside of tepal has broad central crimson stripe with silvery edge. Inside of tepal is crimson. Anthers are crimson and carpels are prominent and white.

GROUP XI
THE ORIENTALIS GROUP
The Yellow Group

In the other groups yellow colouring is seldom seen. Here they are all in shades of yellow. All easy to grow and coming when you need colour in the garden. They are very difficult to classify. We gardeners need only remember the names of the best. They are blessed with fine foliage and the best seed heads of any group.

Flowering time:	From early summer into autumn.
Size:	Can make very large plants. 'Helios' is an exception.
Strength:	Hardy. Reliable.
Flowers:	A profusion of flowers of shades of yellow and in the form of lanterns, nodding bells, or open bells. Usually four tepals. Silky seedheads may form at same time as flowers or later. *Clematis rehderiana* is scented.
Care:	Plant as any other shrub. Small plants can be pruned to ground in late winter. For a large plant prune side shoots back to the main stem in late winter.
Uses:	To cover walls, fences, arches, pergolas. Climbing into small trees and shrubs. 'Helios' in borders.
Points for:	Brings yellow into garden. Hardy. Strong. Seed heads. Easy to grow and propagate. Free of stem rot (clematis wilt).
Points against:	Need space.
Hardiness ratings:	USA – Zone 4–9. Worldwide – annual average minimum temp. above –34°C (–30°F).

A *Clematis tangutica* climbs high on a wall at Burford House Gardens, Tenbury, UK.

'Bill Mackenzie'

An excellent plant, the most popular in this group. Flowers for a long time. Seed heads continue to turn of the year. Bloom and seed heads come together. Can cover an area of 20sq.ft. (6sq.m).

'Aureolin'

Makes a fine plant up to 10ft. (3m.). Very reliable. Very productive of flowers. Fine seed heads.

'Helios'

A plant for a small garden. Grows to 5ft. (1.5m.). Starts growth early for this group — early summer. Nodding flower opens flat. Scented. Covered with flowers and seed heads.

'Golden Tiara' (syn. 'Kugotia')

Vigorous plant for late summer and early autumn. Nodding flowers with dark purple centre. Excellent silvery seed heads. Up to 10ft. (3m.) in height.

Clematis rehderiana

Different from previous clematis in this group as it has pale yellow nodding bells that hang in clusters. Scented. Can make a very big plant, up to 20ft. (6m.). Spectacular if given plenty of room.

Dew on 'Bill MacKenzie'.

Seed heads

Frost on a *Clematis tangutica*.

Clematis orientalis.

GROUP XII
LATE GROUP
The Autumn Group

The clematis year ends with a mixed group of large vigorous plants that take you into the autumn. The wild European clematis *Clematis vitalba* ('Old Man's Beard') belongs to this group. As there is less light at this time of the year, for good flowering plant in sunny sheltered parts of the garden. *Clematis terniflora* takes you into November and already *Clematis napaulensis* from Group I may be in bloom in your conservatory and so starting next year's cycle.

Flowering time:	May start in midsummer but go on into the autumn.
Size:	Most make large plants and 'Western Virgin' is a giant.
Strength:	Most very hardy.
Flowers:	All produce showers of small flowers, some scented.
Leaves:	Variable.
Care:	Plant as any shrub. Plant in sunny sheltered positions. Prune small plants to the ground in late winter. Prune branches of large plants back to main stems.
Uses:	On walls, fences, arches, pergolas. Into trees and large shrubs. As some will smother small trees or shrubs, match with care.
Points for:	Colour in autumn. Vigour. Scent. Free of stem rot (clematis wilt).
Points against:	Need space.
Hardiness ratings:	USA Zone 3-9. Worldwide – average minimum temp. above -40°C (-40°F).

Clematis vitalba the wild European plant belongs to this group and is seen here in autumn, clothing trees with its seed heads.

Clematis x *triternata* 'Rubromarginata'

Do not be put off by the name. This is a wonderful plant. A plant for every garden. Much hardier than its parent *Clematis flammula*, it is covered with myriads of flowers – but here with a red margin that makes a most attractive small flower. Powerful hawthorn scent. Can make 20ft. (6m.). (Triternata = triternate leaves. Rubromarginata = red margin.)

'Paul Farges'

Sometimes called 'Summer Snow' for the abundance of small white flowers. A very strong plant, up to 20ft. (6m.). With no pruning it starts flowering in early summer and goes on into autumn. With pruning starts flowering in midsummer.

'Western Virgin'

If you want an autumn montana then this is it. From Manitoba, Canada, it can stand cold conditions. Very vigorous and needs a large tree as host.

Clematis terniflora

This plant takes us into late autumn. A splendid finale to the clematis year. Vigorous up to 20ft. (6m.) covered with clusters of white, sweet smelling, flowers. Sometimes known as 'Sweet Autumn'. Needs a sunny sheltered position in cold areas. Reliable in warm climates. Can be so late flowering as to find itself in snow – as here. (Terniflora = flowers in threes.)

BUYING YOUR CLEMATIS

The Choice Available
Clematis are sold in three styles:

1. A mature two-year-old plant, usually in a 2-litre pot, that can be put into the ground right away (See Plate I). As long as the ground is not frozen the clematis can be planted any time of the year. The best time to plant it, and the time when most plants are sold, is the spring. The plant comes to life at that time and responds to the warm earth. Another good time is the early autumn so that the plant is established before the winter.

    How do you tell a good plant? Firstly, look at the foliage. Are the leaves clean and healthy looking? Check the bottom of the pot. Are the roots visible through the bottom hole? If so, that is a good sign. If in doubt ask the staff to tip the plant out of the pot. You can now check the roots. Are there any insects or larvae on the roots? If so reject the plant. Being 'pot bound' is not often a problem with clematis.

    With the Early Large Flowered, Group VI apply special care. Check the stems. You need a plant with two or more stems. The more the better. Why? Should one stem be attacked by stem rot (clematis wilt) then the others will survive and give you flowers.

Plate I. A healthy mature two year old plant in a 6½in. (16.5cm.) pot is ready for planting.

2. A first year plant is termed a 'liner' in the trade (See Plate II). They can be just as healthy as a mature plant but they need another year before they can be planted. They have the advantage of being much cheaper. But you wait longer for the bloom. To these you must do two things:-

a) Prune it. Prune by cutting the stem or stems above the node nearest to the ground. The node is the bump on the stem where leaves emerge. This will have the effect of stimulating the plant to throw up more stems from the crown and so make a stronger plant.

110

b) Repot in a 6½in. (16½cm.) diameter pot. Use a good compost. If in doubt use John Innes No. 3. Mix in a teaspoonful of long acting fertiliser or a small lump of long acting fertiliser – but keep well away from the centre of the plant. Fit pot with a 3ft. (1m.) cane. Where will you put this plant? If you have a greenhouse you can keep it there for a year. But a better place for it is the ground. At a sheltered corner of the garden sink it into the ground with soil up to and covering the top edge. It will be snug there until mature enough to plant. Only in very dry periods need you water it. Do not water it at all in the winter. As it makes long stems tie them to the cane. These long stems can also be pruned to above their first node. Do not produce flowers during this year, concentrate on making a strong plant.

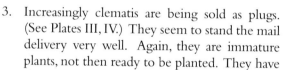

Plate II. A 'liner' in a 3½in. (8 cm.) pot needs repotting, pruning and keeping for a year.

3. Increasingly clematis are being sold as plugs. (See Plates III, IV.) They seem to stand the mail delivery very well. Again, they are immature plants, not then ready to be planted. They have the advantage, like a liner, of being cheap but needing to be looked after for a year. Plant in a 6½in. (16½cm.) pot. Prune as with a 'liner' and then put pot into the ground for a year, or until root system fills the pot and the plant is strong. Care for it as with 'liners'.

Plate III. A plug travels comfortably in its plastic shell.

Plate IV. The immature first year plant needs potting in a 6½in. (16.5 cm.) pot and keeping a year.

Repotting (See below)

1. First, put some compost into a large pot, then place the small pot (with the clematis) inside the large pot to see if both edges are level. If not, add more peat or compost at the bottom until the edge of the inner pot is level with that of the edge of the outer one.
2. Add compost all round the small pot, firming it down gently until the large pot is filled to the brim.
3. You now take the small pot out from inside the large one.
4. Holding the small pot with the clematis in the left hand, slip the base of the stems between the fingers of your right hand, invert the pot and cane, tap the pot edge gently on the edge of a bench or on the top of a fork stuck in the ground (or tap edge of pot with a stick).
5. The clematis will immediately slip out of its pot.
6. The clematis will now fit perfectly into the space previously made in the larger pot. Gently firm and the job is done.

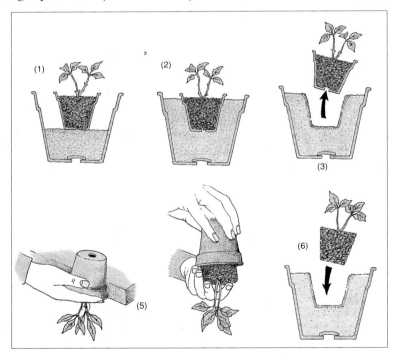

Repotting made easy.

Traditionally, it is usual to repot by using a sequence of pots increasing in size. This practice is now being questioned as, after an initial hesitation, plants grow quickly and well in large pots.

Sources for plants

The first point of purchase for many plants is the internet. Contact my website (www.howells98.freeserve.com.uk) and there you will find a list of British nurseries who do mail order business in Europe and the world. You can also approach the website of specialist nurseries in Holland, Germany, France, Japan, USA and the UK. Contact PLANT FINDER (www.rhs.org.uk) also P.P.P. INDEX for Europe.

Many will visit a specialist clematis nursery. Often the owner developed an interest in the plant as a gardener, loves it and moved into growing and selling it. They know their plant. Advice is possible but not of course a long lecture. There will be a large choice of plants but buy the one you decided at home that you needed or you will be the victim of 'impulse buying'. All the nurseries will have their own informative catalogues that you can study at home and they often have a display garden.

Garden centres often have a good choice of the most popular clematis although the choice will be less than that at a specialist nursery. Also they are less likely to have the unusual. Naturally, advice is likely to be more superficial than in the specialist nursery. Some nurseries and outlets sell 'liners' alone. These may be a satisfactory choice but be aware that you have the care of it for at least a year before you can plant it.

Your rights

Most countries will have laws that define the customer's rights. In the UK for instance, under the Sale of Goods Act 1979, all plants must:

1. Fit their description, e.g. be correctly labelled.
2. Be of merchantable quality, e.g. the clematis must be healthy.
3. Be reasonably fit for their purpose, e.g. if the clematis was bought as suitable for a certain climate then it should be so.

STARTING A COLLECTION

Many gardeners want a collection of clematis as part of a larger collection of other plants. Some intend to make clematis their main interest (clematarians). A few become so enthusiastic as to collect rare and unusual clematis.

The key to successful collecting is to know your groups. This can easily be done. Just **twelve** clematis, one in each group, will tell you about all **twelve** groups and hence all clematis. I would suggest the following **twelve** for your first collection:

Group I	Evergreen	*armandii* 'Apple Blossom'
Group II	Alpina	'Blue Dancer'
Group III	Macropetala	'Markham's Pink'
Group IV	Montana	'Mayleen' – large area
		'Freda' – small area
Group V	Rockery	'Joe'
Group VI	Early Large	'Lasurstern'
Group VII	Late Large	'Victoria'
Group VIII	Herbaceous	*integrifolia* 'Rosea'
Group IX	Viticella	'Etoile Violette'
Group X	Texensis	'Princess Diana'
Group XI	Orientalis	'Bill MacKenzie'
Group XII	Late	x *triternata* 'Rubromarginata'

You may wish to start with an easy one. So try the viticella 'Etoile Violette'. 'Victoria' in Group VII is also easy and reliable. In the spring, Montana Group IV will make an immediate appeal – say 'Mayleen' or 'Freda'. You fill in with the rest of the groups and then end with *armandii* Group I, which needs a warm sheltered place out of the wind. If it takes, it will give you endless winter joy.

As each plant grows read about the group here. You will soon know all the groups and know which especially appeals to you and suits your garden. So you will have your own unique collection.

Some clematis are happy in semi-shade but the same plant will always do better in a sunny aspect. On your patio you may not have a choice of putting them in the soil and so a container it must be. If you have a choice put it in the soil. The plant will give more bloom, the roots will want less water under the paving, you will have less watering to do, and can leave your plants unattended for a couple of weeks when you have a holiday. It is better, however, to have a clematis in a container than no clematis at all.

UNDERSTANDING STEM ROT – 'CLEMATIS WILT'

New knowledge has brought hope of managing clematis wilt. We now know that only one group of clematis out of twelve is vulnerable; another group occasionally wilts but too rarely to need treatment. Ten groups are entirely wilt free. Furthermore, the fungus almost never kills a plant. Ignorance fuels alarm, understanding brings promise.

The Enemy

Faced with an opponent, it helps to know that opponent. Better still put yourself in the place of the enemy – in this case a tiny fungus – *phoma clematidina*.

This little chap can only feed on clematis. For centuries it had a thin time. Then Jackman in 1860 hybridised 'Jackmanii'. This beautiful plant had such an impact that clematis took off. By 1880 Jackman had over 400 new clematis in his catalogue. Other nurseries followed all over Europe. Now the tiny *phoma* never had it so good. The best way to start an epidemic is to pack people together. The same applies to clematis. As the clematis were packed together the 'wilt' spread and spread so that it brought the industry to a halt by 1880. But the gardeners and growers then had little notion of germs and fungi. Now we do.

The Fungus

Gloyer, a scientist in New York State, USA, discovered the fungus in 1915. His finding was ignored until recently when it was confirmed in the UK, Holland and New Zealand. But there was another conundrum. Working with a group of expert gardeners and growers I found some years ago that the fungus only attacks one group of clematis – the Early Large Flowered group with clematis such as 'Nelly Moser', 'Elsa Späth', 'Countess of Lovelace', 'W.E. Gladstone', etc. This finding was confirmed recently by research at the University of Derby. So why is this group vulnerable? I found that it was because *C. lanuginosa*, the woolly clematis, from China had been extensively used as a parent in the last century. *C. lanuginosa* is very vulnerable to wilting and it has parented most of the clematis in the Early Large Flowered group, the vulnerable group. (A lesser culprit was *C. fortunei*, probably contaminated by *C. lanuginosa*.)

How It Destroys

All fungi need moisture for growth. It also likes a warm day, ideally about 70°F (23°C). It starts its growth on a leaf. Any clematis leaf in any group can be used by the fungus. On the leaf it makes a brown patch which extends down the stalk to the node on the green stem where the stalk starts. Ten of the clematis groups in my classification repel the invader. The eleventh – the Late Large Flowered group – partly repels the invader. The twelfth – the Early Large Flowered group (with *C. lanuginosa* in its background) – cannot defend itself and in goes the fungus. (See Fig.3)

Once in, the fungus destroys an area of about an inch either side of the node. This rots and turns black, jet-black. That is why it would be better for us to talk of 'stem rot' rather than 'wilt'. 'Stem rot' tells us what is happening inside our clematis.

The fungus does so much damage because it destroys right across the stem. The sap coming up the stem is unable to get past the node so the stem above withers (wilts) and turns brown – just as if you had cut across the stem. You can see this clearly in the first photograph ever taken of stem rot. (See Plate V)

The fungus finds young green stems much easier to attack. As the plant gets older and the stems get woody and brown it is more difficult for the fungus to get into the stem. Then it will only attack the green branches of the brown stems and do much less damage.

What can you do?

The most obvious thing you can do is to buy a good plant in the vulnerable Group VI, the Early Large Flowered, with more than one stem. If you lose one, the others will still prosper and flower.

It was thought that to plant deep would encourage roots to strike on nodes below the soil surface and make extra plants. So if you lost the main plant you might have a subsidiary plant. But what you have done is to pull a node or nodes into the top of the soil where the ideal moist conditions for fungus growth exists. Therefore, do not plant deep. Plant at the normal depth for a shrub, leaving the nodes above soil level. Buy a good plant with several stems.

Reduce moisture by encouraging drainage at the collar of the plant with a 3in. (7.5cm.) layer of sand or grit at the bottom of the stem. If you can, use a leaky pipe watering 4in. (10cm.) below the surface. Avoid watering the leaves. Water into the soil away from the collar of the plant.

If wilt strikes cut across the stem below the affected node. This is often the

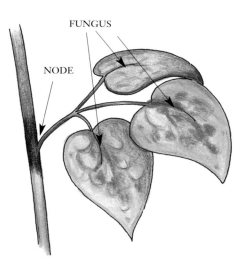

FUNGUS

NODE

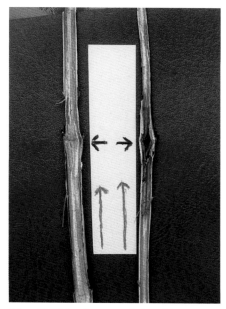

Figure 3. The fungus grows on a leaf surface, makes a brown patch, and then makes its way down the stalk of the leaf to enter the stem by a node. It destroys an area, right across the stem, on each side of the node. This area is black. No sap can pass this area and so the stem above the node dies.

Plate V. This photograph is of 'stem rot' (wilt) in clematis. Two clematis nodes (marked with black arrows) are seen here. The flow of sap upwards is indicated by red arrows. The left node has healthy green tissue above and below it (the flow of sap keeps it healthy). The right node has healthy green tissue below it but at the node itself this tissue has been destroyed by the fungus leaving a black mass for about 2in. (5cm.). Above the right node the tissue is cut off from nourishment by the black fungal mass and this tissue wilts and turns brown as it dies.

lowest node on the stem or the next three above. This will be the lowest node that has no leaves coming out of it. After the cut, the stem top that you leave in the soil will be green, so you know you are in healthy tissue. Burn the brown stem as it has fungus on it. It is at the next stage that the plant dies. It is you who could kill it by assuming the roots are dead! They are alive but need water. Keep looking after the plant and in a few days new shoots will appear from below the soil. The fungus pruned the plant for you, but rather too early, and you may miss flowers that summer.

There is no fungicide at the moment recommended for use by gardeners, but a new lot is coming, certainly for the growers. Whether gardeners will use them in this organic world is another matter.

Clematis plants can wither and wilt for other reasons than an attack by this fungus. For example, from the action of your hoe, lack of water, excessive cold or heat, vine weevil at the roots, action by ants, phytophthora, etc.

If you like getting to the bottom of things, then having separated your wilting stem from the plant, put it down on a table and using a razor sharp blade cut lengthways into each node, starting at the bottom node. In one node, often the bottom one, you will now see the black, jet-black, damaged area where the fungus has been at work. (See Plate V.)

Action against stem rot (clematis wilt)

1. In the Early Large Flowered Group, Group VI, buy a plant with several stems. This is important.
2. Do not plant deep.
3. Water by using a seepy hose if possible. Avoid overhead watering.
4. If disaster strikes (a) check to see if there is a simple cause (b) cut the stem off below the damaged node and destroy.
5. Keep watering your plant.
6. If fungicides become available use every month in the growing season and change the fungicide every season at least.
7. If disappointment continues, grow the wilt-free groups, especially Group IX the Viticella Group.

FURTHER READING

Howells, J. 'Clematis Wilt. A Review of the Literature'. *The Plantsman,* 15, p.148. (1993)
'Vulnerability to Clematis Wilt'. *The Clematis,* p. 51. (1994)
'The Genetic Background of Wilting Clematis'. *The Clematis,* p. 62. (1994)
'The Lesion of Stem Rot'. *The Clematis,* p. 53. (1996)

A mixture of viticellas make a riot of colour.

Pronunciation

It is more important to be understood than to abide by the finer points of pronunciation.

As all the authorities (*Oxford Dictionary, Webster's Dictionary, Fowler's English Usage*) are agreed, there is no difficulty with this name. We can consider it under three syllables:

cle   has a short 'e' and the syllable is pronounced
               KLE as in 'cleric'
ma–   'a' is a short 'a' as in 'apart'
'tis   'i' is short and 'tis' rhymes with 'hiss'

For clematis we have: kle ma tis

Plural is clematises but its awkwardness has led to its being discarded. Therefore 'clematis' is used for one or more than one plant.

A clematarian is a gardener enthusiastic about growing clematis.

A clematarium is a garden largely for growing clematis.

HARDINESS RATINGS

USA

In the USA a convenient zonal system for plant hardiness has been developed by the United States Department of Agriculture (USDA). This divides the country into 11 zones depending on the annual minimum temperature for each zone. See Table I which gives the average minimum temperature for each zone.

At Table II will be found the zones appropriate for optimum growth in each clematis Group. The lowest number indicates the zone with the lowest temperature for survival. Clematis will not usually thrive in Zones 1 and 2, without special care. The highest number indicates the zone with the highest temperature for reliable growth; this is usually Zone 9 for clematis. Clematis can adapt to Zones 10 and 11, given suitable micro climates.

An American gardener will usually know the zone to which his garden belongs. When considering climatic conditions appropriate to growing a particular clematis find to which Group the plant belongs. Table II will then give you the zones in which you can grow that Group. You will then know whether that plant can be grown in your zone and your garden, e.g. 'Nelly Moser' belongs to Group VI. It can usually be grown in your garden if the garden is in zones 4-9. From the Table II it will be seen that particular care is required with Group I, Evergreen, Group IV, Rockery and Group V, Montana.

World-wide

From the tables I and II it is also possible to establish world-wide ratings. Knowing the annual minimum temperature for your area in the world you can find your zone in Table I. For example, consulting Table I, an annual minimum temperature for your area below -40°C puts you in Zone 2. Consulting Table II you can see that it makes it difficult for you to grow any group of clematis. Whereas a minimum temperature of -14°C puts you in zone 7 in Table I and you can grow clematis in the Group V, Montana Group and Group IV, Rockery Group with care, and clematis in all the other groups. Consulting Table I again, a minimum annual temperature of -9°C puts you in zone 8 and you can grow all groups of clematis, whereas a minimum annual temperature of 5°C puts you in zone 11 and it will be too hot for most clematis to thrive in your garden.

A Reminder

A gardener must also take account of the microclimate in his garden which may differ from the zone rating for that area because of elevation, closeness to the sea or lakes, prevailing winds, rainfall, humidity, frost pockets, etc. The unsuitability of a zone for a particular plant may sometimes be corrected by bringing the plant indoors in winter.

TABLE I

Zone		Fahrenheit	Celsius
Zone	1	below –50°	below –45°
Zone	2	–50° to –40°	–45° to –40°
Zone	3	–40° to –30°	–40° to –34°
Zone	4	–30° to –20°	–34° to –29°
Zone	5	–20° to –10°	–29° to –23°
Zone	6	–10° to 0°	–23° to –18°
Zone	7	0° to 10°	–18° to –12°
Zone	8	10° to 20°	–12° to –7°
Zone	9	20° to 30°	–7° to –1°
Zone	10	30°to 40°	–1° to 4°
Zone	11	Above 40°	Above 4°

TABLE II

		USA	World–Wide (Minimum Winter Temp.)
Group I	Evergreen	Zone 6-9	Above –23°C
Group II	Alpina	Zone 3-9	Above –40°C
Group III	Macropetala	Zone 3-9	Above –40°C
Group IV	Montana	Zone 7-9	Above –18°C
Group V	Rockery	Zone 7-9	Above –18°C
Group VI	Early Large Flowered	Zone 4-9	Above –34°C
Group VII	Late Large Flowered	Zone 3-9	Above –40°C
Group VIII	Herbaceous	Zone 3-9	Above –40°C
Group IX	Viticella	Zone 3-9	Above –40°C
Group X	Texensis	Zone 4-9	Above –34°C
Group XI	Orientalis	Zone 4-9	Above –34°C
Group XII	Late	Zone 3-9	Above –40°C

A young 'Victoria' climbs strongly into holly.

Rose 'Iceberg' and clematis
'Princess of Wales' make an attractive pair

LISTS OF USEFUL CLEMATIS

WHITE CLEMATIS

GROUP I EVERGREEN	*armandii, armandii* 'Snowdrift', *cirrhosa, napaulensis, paniculata.*
GROUP II ALPINA	'White Columbine', 'White Moth'.
GROUP III MACROPETALA	'White Swan', 'Snowbird', 'White Lady'.
GROUP IV MONTANA	'Alexander', 'Elten', 'Jenny Keay', 'Peveril', 'Pleniflora', *montana, chrysocoma,* 'Grandiflora'.
GROUP VI ROCKERY	'Joe', 'Early Sensation'.
GROUP VI EARLY LARGE	'Duchess of Edinburgh', 'Marie Boisselot', 'Edith', 'Miss Bateman', 'Snow Queen', 'Sylvia Denny', 'Valge Daam', 'John Paul II'.
GROUP VII LATE LARGE	'John Huxtable', 'Jackmanii Alba', x *jouiniana* 'Praecox', 'Mrs Robert Brydon'.
GROUP VIII HERBACEOUS	*recta, integrifolia* 'Alba', 'Sander'.
GROUP IX VITICELLA	'Alba Luxurians', 'Huldine', *campaniflora,* 'Little Nell'.
GROUP X TEXENSIS	
GROUP XI ORIENTALIS	
GROUP XII LATE GROUP	*vitalba,* 'Paul Farges', 'Western Virgin', *terniflora, flammula.*

Montana 'Grandiflora' climbs into wisteria at Fleur Mille, Guernsey.

YELLOW CLEMATIS

GROUP I EVERGREEN	*chiisanensis.*
GROUP VI ROCKERY	*marmoraria* (Cream), 'Fairy', 'Pixie' (Cream).
GROUP VI EARLY LARGE	'Guernsey Cream', 'Moonlight', 'Lemon Chiffon', 'Wada's Primrose'.
GROUP XI ORIENTALIS	ALL GROUP.

PINK CLEMATIS

GROUP I EVERGREEN	
GROUP II ALPINA	'Rosy Pagoda', 'Pink Flamingo', 'Jacqueline du Pré'.
GROUP III MACROPETALA	'Markham's Pink', 'Rosy O'Grady', 'Willy'.
GROUP IV MONTANA	'Mayleen', 'Vera', 'Rubens', 'Picton's Variety', *chrysocoma* 'Continuity'.
GROUP V ROCKERY	
GROUP VI EARLY LARGE	'Nelly Moser', 'Dr Ruppel', 'Asao', 'Dawn', 'Peveril Pearl'.
GROUP VII LATE LARGE	'Hagley Hybrid', 'Comtesse de Bouchaud', 'Piilu', 'John Warren'.
GROUP VIII HERBACEOUS	'Aljonushka', *integrifolia* 'Rosea'.
GROUP IX VITICELLA	'Minuet', 'Margot Koster', 'Margaret Hunt', 'Pagoda'.
GROUP X TEXENSIS	All shades of pink and red.
GROUP XI ORIENTALIS	
GROUP XII LATE GROUP	

RED CLEMATIS

GROUP I EVERGREEN	
GROUP II ALPINA	'Constance', 'Ruby'.
GROUP III MACROPETALA	
GROUP IV MONTANA	'Freda', 'Broughton Star', 'Warwickshire Rose'.
GROUP V ROCKERY	
GROUP VI EARLY LARGE	'Rouge Cardinal', 'Crimson King', 'Jackmanii Rubra'.
GROUP VII LATE LARGE	'Niobe', 'Madame Edouard André', 'Ernest Markham', 'Voluceau', 'Sunset'.
GROUP VIII HERBACEOUS	
GROUP IX VITICELLA	'Kermesina', 'Purpurea Plena Elegans', 'Royal Velours', 'Ville de Lyon', 'Madame Julia Correvon'. 'Abundance'.
GROUP X TEXENSIS	All shades of pink and red.
GROUP XI ORIENTALIS	
GROUP XII LATE GROUP	

LIGHT BLUE CLEMATIS

GROUP I EVERGREEN	
GROUP II ALPINA	'Columbine', 'Blue Dancer'.
GROUP III MACROPETALA	*macropetala*, 'Ola Howells'.
GROUP IV MONTANA	
GROUP V ROCKERY	
GROUP VI EARLY LARGE	'Lasurstern', 'H.F. Young', 'Fujimusume', 'Mrs Cholmondeley', 'Lawsoniana', 'Liliacina Floribunda', 'Multi Blue'.
GROUP VII LATE LARGE	'Perle d'Azur', 'Prince Charles', 'Ascotiensis'
GROUP VIII HERBACEOUS	'Blue Boy', 'Arabella'.
GROUP IX VITICELLA	'Blue Angel', 'Emilia Plater', 'Betty Corning'.
GROUP X TEXENSIS	
GROUP XI ORIENTALIS	
GROUP XII LATE GROUP	

DARK BLUE CLEMATIS

GROUP I EVERGREEN	
GROUP II ALPINA	'Helsingborg', 'Pamela Jackman'.
GROUP III MACROPETALA	'Jan Lindmark', 'Purple Spider'.
GROUP IV MONTANA	
GROUP V ROCKERY	
GROUP VI EARLY LARGE	'Elsa Späth', 'General Sikorski', 'Richard Pennell', 'Beauty of Worcester', 'Vyvyan Pennell', 'Mrs James Mason'.
GROUP VII LATE LARGE	'Victoria', 'Gipsy Queen', 'Star of India', 'Lady Betty Balfour', 'The Vagabond', 'Jackmanii', 'Luther Burbank', 'Romantika'.
GROUP VIII HERBACEOUS	'Wyevale', PETIT FAUCON, x *aromatica*, 'Durandii', 'Hendersonii'.
GROUP IX VITICELLA	'Etoile Violette', 'Polish Spirit', 'Blue Belle', 'Negritjanka'.
GROUP X TEXENSIS	
GROUP XI ORIENTALIS	
GROUP XII LATE GROUP	

DOUBLE CLEMATIS

GROUP I EVERGREEN	
GROUP II ALPINA	'White Moth'.
GROUP III MACROPETALA	ALL DOUBLE
GROUP IV MONTANA	'Broughton Star', 'Pleniflora', 'Margaret Jones', 'Jenny Keay', 'Marjorie'.
GROUP V ROCKERY	
GROUP VI EARLY LARGE	'Vyvyan Pennell', 'Proteus', ARCTIC QUEEN, 'Duchess of Edinburgh', 'Daniel Deronda', 'Louise Rowe', 'Piilu', 'Mrs Spencer Castle'.
GROUP VII LATE LARGE	'Jackmanii Alba'.
GROUP VIII HERBACEOUS	
GROUP IX VITICELLA	'Purpurea Plena Elegans', 'Flore Plena'.
GROUP X TEXENSIS	
GROUP XI ORIENTALIS	
GROUP XII LATE GROUP	

A clematis of the montana group matches a part of the Ceonathus National Collection, at Eccleston Square, London.

STRIPED CLEMATIS

GROUP VI EARLY LARGE	'Dr Ruppel', 'Nelly Moser', 'Bees' Jubilee', 'Corona', 'Carnaby', 'Capitaine Thuilleaux', 'Barbara Dibley', 'Asao', 'Barbara Jackman', 'Andromeda', 'Piilu'.
GROUP VII LATE LARGE	'Pink Fantasy', 'Star of India'.

SCENTED CLEMATIS

GROUP I EVERGREEN	*armandii* 'Apple Blossom'.
GROUP II ALPINA	'Odorata'.
GROUP III MACROPETALA	
GROUP IV MONTANA	'Elizabeth', 'Mayleen', 'Vera', 'Alexander', 'Picton's Variety', 'Tetrarose', 'Wilsonii'.
GROUP V ROCKERY	
GROUP VI EARLY LARGE	'Fair Rosamond'.
GROUP VII LATE LARGE	
GROUP VIII HERBACEOUS	'Davidiana', 'Sander', 'Wyevale', 'Edward Pritchard', 'Rosea', *recta,* x *aromatica.*
GROUP IX VITICELLA	'Betty Corning', *viticella.*
GROUP X TEXENSIS	*crispa.*
GROUP XI ORIENTALIS	*rehderiana.*
GROUP XII LATE GROUP	C. *flammula,* x *triternata* 'Rubromarginata', *terniflora, vitalba.*

CLEMATIS FOR NORTH ASPECT

GROUP I EVERGREEN	
GROUP II ALPINA	ALL
GROUP III MACROPETALA	ALL
GROUP IV MONTANA	'Grandiflora', 'Mayleen', 'Rubens', *montana*, 'Elizabeth', 'Warwickshire Rose'.
GROUP V ROCKERY	
GROUP VI EARLY LARGE	'Mrs Cholmondeley', 'Nelly Moser', 'W.E. Gladstone', 'Lawsoniana' 'Elsa Späth'.
GROUP VII LATE LARGE	MOST OF THIS GROUP
GROUP VIII HERBACEOUS	MOST OF THIS GROUP
GROUP IX VITICELLA	MOST OF THIS GROUP
GROUP X TEXENSIS	
GROUP XI ORIENTALIS	'Bill Mackenzie'', 'Golden Tiara', 'Aureolin', *rehderiana*
GROUP XII LATE GROUP	x *triternata* 'Rubromarginata', 'Western Virgin', 'Paul Farges'

CLEMATIS FOR CONTAINERS

GROUP I EVERGREEN	UNDER GLASS
GROUP II ALPINA	MOST
GROUP III MACROPETALA	MOST
GROUP IV MONTANA	
GROUP V ROCKERY	'Joe', 'Early Sensation', *marmoraria,* New Zealand hybrids.
GROUP VI EARLY LARGE	'Lasurstern', 'Nelly Moser', 'Miss Bateman', 'Asao', 'Dawn', 'H.F. Young', 'Snow Queen', 'Andromeda'.
GROUP VII LATE LARGE	'Comtesse de Bouchaud', 'Hagley Hybrid', 'John Huxtable', 'The Vagabond', 'Niobe', 'Pink Fantasy', 'Prince Charles', 'Twilight'.
GROUP VIII HERBACEOUS	ALL FORMS OF INTEGRIFOLIA
GROUP IX VITICELLA	'Huldine', 'Ville de Lyon', 'Margot Koster'.
GROUP X TEXENSIS	ALL
GROUP XI ORIENTALIS	'Helios'.
GROUP XII LATE GROUP	

'Wada's Primrose' and 'Broughton Star' decorate a pergola.

INDEX

Page numbers in **bold** denote illustrations.

THE TWELVE CLEMATIS GROUPS

Alpina Group – single bells – early spring flowering

Early Large Flowered Group – 'dinner plate' – early summer

142